This book
belongs to:

Kaitlyn Grace Guiser

_____

_____

December 1995

Merry Christmas Katie ♥♥♥

All our love,
Uncle Morgan, Aunt Debbie,
"M.J." and Jason

The Story of Christmas

ILLUSTRATED BY FREYA TANZ

THE REGINA PRESS
New York

A very long time ago, a young girl named Mary lived in the city of Nazareth. One day, an angel of God came to Mary. The angel told Mary that God had chosen her to be the mother of His Son, Jesus.

While Mary was expecting this special child, the King said that all families had to return to their birthplace to register for taxes. Mary's husband, Joseph, was from Bethlehem, so they began the long journey.

They were very tired when they finally arrived. The city was crowded with other travelers and there was no room at the inn. Mary and Joseph settled in a stable. The baby Jesus was born that night and Mary laid Him in a manger.

That same night, the shepherds were watching their sheep in the hills overlooking Bethlehem. Suddenly, the dark night sky filled with a bright heavenly light.

An angel appeared to the frightened shepherds.
The angel said, "Do not be afraid, for I bring you
good news of great joy. Tonight in Bethlehem,
a child is born who is Christ the Lord!"

The shepherds found the baby Jesus in the small stable. They knelt before Him and were filled with joy.

Far away in the east, three wise men saw a bright new star shining in the sky. They followed the star to Bethlehem. The star was shining over the stable where they found the baby Jesus.

The wise men knelt before the baby Jesus. They gave him gifts of gold, frankincense, and myrrh. The stable was filled with joy and love that spread throughout the ages.